World Champion

MINNESOTA TWINS TRIVIA

Jack Clary

QUINLAN PRESS
Boston

To my nephew Greg Roman, who learned from Kirby Puckett that an athlete can be far bigger than his size.

ACKNOWLEDGEMENTS

I would like to thank Pat Kelly of the Pro Baseball Hall of Fame, Ginny Greene of the *St. Paul Pioneer Press & Dispatch,* Julie Anne Stevens of Kasson, Minnesota, and my editor at Quinlan Press, Kevin Stevens, for their help with this book.

Jack Clary is a free-lance sports media specialist and author of over two dozen sports books, including *Baseball's Signs and Symbols, Jim Palmer's Way to Fitness,* and *Once a Giant, Always...* (with Andy Robustelli). For fifteen years he was a sportswriter and columnist for *The Associated Press,* the *New York World Telegram & Sun* and the Boston Herald Traveler.

TABLE OF CONTENTS

Washington Senators

1. What were the seasons in which the old Washington Senators, predecessors of the Twins, represented the American League in the Nation's Capital?

2. What Washington Senators pitcher holds the major league record for hitting the most batsmen during his career?

3. Who was the Washington Senators player who led the American League five consecutive years in stolen bases (1939 to 1943)?

4. Who was the Senators first baseman who was the last to win a pair of American League batting titles?

5. Who was the only pitcher elected to Baseball's Hall of Fame at its inception?

6. How many games did Walter Johnson win for the Senators during his 21 seasons?

7. How many seasons did Walter Johnson lead the American League in strikeouts?

8. In 1959 the American League had dual home run kings. Who were they and how many homers did they hit?

9. In 1954 Idaho Sen. Clayton Welker recommended what future Hall-of-Famer to Senators' owner Calvin Griffith.

10. What was pitcher Walter Johnson's famous nickname when he pitched for the Senators?

11. During Walter Johnson's career, he walked 100 or more batters during how many seasons?
    a) 5
    b) 1
    c) 3
    d) 9

12. In how many seasons did Walter Johnson win 20 or more games?
    a) 12   c) 10
    b) 9   d) 14

13. Who was the manager of the 1924-1925 American League champion Senators who was known as the "Boy Wonder"?

14. This former Senators catcher later became a renowned author and master spy for the U.S. Government. Who was he?

15. This former Senators player became one of the few in baseball history whose major league career touched four different decades. Name him.

16. How much were the Washington Senators paid by Boston owner Tom Yawkey for shortstop Joe Cronin?

17. Who managed the Washington Senators when they won the 1933 American League pennant?

18. Though Joe Cronin made much of his fame playing with the Senators, which major league team signed him to his first pro contract?

19. Who was the Washington Senators pitcher who became known as "The Clown Prince of Baseball"?

20. Who was the Senators outfielder, now in the Hall of Fame, who led the 1925 World Series in hitting and had a lifetime .322 average?

21. Who were the only two Washington Senators ever to win the American League RBI title?

22. Who was the only Senators player ever to win the American League home run title outright?

23. What 1924 Senators player shares the World Series record for reaching base on seven consecutive at-bats?

24. How old was Walter Johnson when he pitched his record-setting seventh opening day shutout victory in 1926?

25. Who was the Washington catcher who once threw out eight base-stealers in one game?

26. What Hall-of-Fame pitcher was the co-founder of the American League and in 1912 became owner of the Washington Senators?

27. How many strikeouts did Walter Johnson record during his career with the Washington Senators?

28. Who was the Senators third baseman who set an American League record with 28 home runs as leadoff batter?

29. Who was the Senators first baseman/out-fielder who hit home runs in six consecutive games?

30. Who were the only two Senators ever selected as the American League Most Valuable Players?

31. Who were the two Washington Senators players selected to play in the first All-Star Game in 1933?

32. Who was the Senators pitcher who, after winning the opening game in front of the President, coined the famous saying, "When the President of the United States comes out to see Ol' Bobo pitch, Ol' Bobo ain't gonna let him down"?

33. What was the outcome of the Washington Senators' World Series against the New York Giants in 1933?

34. What was the outcome of the Washington Senators' World Series appearance in 1925?

35. When was the Washington Senators' first World Series appearance and what was the outcome?

36. What Senators players were picked in consecutive years as American League Rookies of the Year?

37. Who were the only two pitchers ever to hurl a no-hit game for the Washington Senators?

38. Who was the batboy on the Washington Senators' 1924 World Series championship team?

39. How many times did Babe Ruth and Walter Johnson oppose each other as pitchers, and what was their record?

Answers

1. The Senators played in Washington from 1901 to 1960.

2. Walter Johnson (ouch!) hit 206 batters during his 21-season career.

3. George Case of the Senators won the AL base-stealing title five straight seasons.

4. Mickey Vernon won the AL batting title in 1946 (.353) and 1953 (.337).

5. Walter Johnson

6. Walter Johnson had 416 victories during his Senators career.

7.   Johnson was the AL's strikeout leader for 12 of his 21 major league seasons.

8.   Harmon Killebrew of the Senators tied Rocky Colavito of the Indians with 42 home runs.

9.   Welker recommended Harmon Killebrew, a native of Payette, Idaho.

10.   Johnson was known as "Big Train."

11.   b) Johnson walked 100 or more batters only once, in 1916.

12.   a) twelve times with 20 or more wins

13.   Bucky Harris earned that nickname.

14.   Moe Berg, who caught pitcher Walter Johnson during some of his greatest seasons

15.   Jim Kaat, who began his major league career with the Washington Senators in 1959.

16.   Cronin was dealt to the Red Sox in 1935 for $250,000, the highest price ever paid for a player to that time.

17.   Joe Cronin

18. The Pittsburgh Pirates signed Cronin in 1925.

19. Al Schact, whose greatest fame came after he retired when he entertained millions with his antics

20. Sam Rice, who spent 19 years with the Senators.

21. Goose Goslin (129) in 1924 and Roy Sievers (114) in 1957

22. Roy Sievers hit 42 in 1957.

23. Goose Goslin, in 1924

24. Johnson was 41 years old.

25. Charlie Farrell nailed eight base-stealers in a game played May 11, 1897.

26. Clark Griffith

27. Johnson struck out 3,508 batters.

28. Eddie Yost, who played 15 seasons with the Senators in the forties and fifties.

29. Roy Sievers did it between July 29 and August 3, 1957.

30. Walter Johnson in 1924 and shortstop Roger Peckinpaugh in 1925

31.   Shortstop Joe Cronin and pitcher Alvin Crowder represented the Senators in the first All-Star Game.

32.   Louis (Bobo) Newsome, after shutting out the Yankees, 1-0

33.   They lost to the Giants, 4 games to 1.

34.   They lost to the Pittsburgh Pirates, 4 games to 3.

35.   They defeated the New York Giants, 4 games to 3, in 1924.

36.   Outfielders Albie Pearson (1958) and Bob Allison (1959)

37.   Walter Johnson defeated the Red Sox, 1-0, on July 1, 1920; and Bob Burke beat Boston, 5-0, on August 8, 1931.

38.   Former Twins owner Calvin Griffith, whose father, Clark, owned the team.

39.   Ruth and Johnson faced each other nine times, and Ruth won six, three by 1-0 shutouts.

Hitters

1. Which Twins players hold the team record for consecutive hits?

2. What Twins player accumulated the most total bases in a single game?

3. Which Twins player tied a major league record with three triples in one game?

4. Who was the Twins player who became the ninth player in major league history to get four hits in his first big league game?

5. Do you remember Gary Gaetti's first game at the Metrodome and what he did?

6. How many Twins players had two or more

hits in a game against the Indians in 1975 that tied an American League record?

7. Which Twins player had the most pinch hits in a single season?

8. Which Twins player has the most lifetime four-hit games?

9. This Twins infielder hit just .290 in his senior year in high school yet wound up as an All-SEC shortstop before signing with the Twins.

10. What Twins player holds the AL record for leading the league in triples in consecutive seasons, and how many?

11. What Twins hitter shares the American League record for leading the league in hits over consecutive years, and how many years did he accomplish the feat?

12. Which Twins rookie holds the record for achieving the most hits in his first major league season?

13. What Twins player holds the record for reaching base safely in a single season?

14. What Twins hitter has the highest batting average ever for a rookie player?

Hitters—Questions

15. What Twins hitter holds the rookie record for most at-bats?

16. Which Twins hitter holds the American League record for most at-bats for a left-handed hitter in a single season?

17. Rod Carew hit the most triples in Twins history. How many?
    a) 110
    b) 121
    c) 103
    d) 90

18. Rod Carew is the Twins' all-time hit-leader with:
    a) 2,274
    b) 2,225
    c) 2,085
    d) 2,162

19. Tony Oliva is the Twins' all-time leader in doubles. He hit:
    a) 329
    b) 342
    c) 298
    d) 386

20. Who was the first Twins player to get five hits in one game?

21. Who is credited with the longest hitting streak in Twins history?

22. Who was the first Twins player to hit in 20 or more straight games?

23. Which Twins player has the all-time best career batting mark?

24. Which current Twins player is credited with the longest hitting streak?

25. Which Twins player has scored the most runs in the team's history?

26. Which Twins player has had the most at-bats in the team's history?

27. Which Twins player accumulated the most total bases in the team's history?

28. Which Twins player hit the most singles in the team's history?

29. Which Twins player has the highest single-season batting mark?

30. Which current Twins player also had the most at-bats and plate appearances in a single season in club history, and how many did he have?

31. Which player in Twins history holds the club record for the most hits in a single season?

32. This current Twins player also holds the all-time pinch-hitting average record for a single season. Who is he?

33. Who holds the Twins' single-season record for most bunt hits?

34. In 1977 Rod Carew set five team hitting records, including how many triples that season?

35. Who holds the Twins' record for most two-base hits during a single season?

36. Who holds the team record for the most multi-hit games in a single season?

37. Which Twins player holds the record for leading the team in hitting for the most seasons, and what is that number?

38. Which Twins player has led the American League the most times in hitting, and how often did he do it?

39. Which Twins player holds the record for leading the team in consecutive batting titles, and how many times did he do it?

40. Who has the team record for the most four-or-more-hit games, and how many did he have?

41. Can you name the Twins players who have hit for the cycle (single-double-triple-HR)?

42. Who was the first Twins player ever to hit for the cycle?

43. Which Twins player has appeared in the most All-Star Games?

44. How many four-or-more-hit games did Tony Oliva have during his Twins career?

45. Who is second to Rod Carew in leading the Twins in hitting, and in how many seasons?

46. Who was the first Twins player ever to hit four extra-base hits in a single game?

47. Which great Twins hitter never played high school baseball but was picked off the sandlots?

48. What hitter holds the Twins record for getting five hits in a game, and how many times did he do it?

Answers

1. Tony Oliva (1967) and Mickey Hatcher (1985) each had nine consecutive hits for a Twins record.

2. Tim Teufel had 13 total bases in a game against Toronto on September 16, 1983.

3. Ken Landreaux hit three triples in a game against Texas on July 3, 1980.

4. Kirby Puckett slammed four hits in his major league debut against the Angels in 1984.

5. In his first Twins game at the Metrodome, Gaetti hit two home runs and just missed a third when he was tagged out at home

plate trying for an inside-the-park homer; and he also had four RBIs.

6. Nine Twins had two or more hits in a game against Cleveland on August 16, 1975, to tie an AL mark.

7. Rich Morales was successful on 14 pinch-hitting tries in 1978.

8. Rod Carew had eight four-hit games in his career to lead all Twins players.

9. Steve Lombardozzi hit just .290 in his senior year at Buccholz HS in Gainesville, Florida.

10. Zoilo Versalles led the AL in triples three straight years (1963-1965), though he tied for the lead in 1964-1965.

11. Tony Oliva led the AL for three straight seasons in hits (1964-1966).

12. Tony Oliva's 217 is the American League record for most hits by a rookie.

13. Rod Carew got on base 311 times in 1977, most ever by any Twins player.

14. Tony Oliva's .323 in 1964 was the best ever for a rookie.

15. Tony Oliva set a record by going to bat 672 times in 1964.

16. Tony Oliva's 672 in 1964 was also an AL record for left-handers.

17. d

18. c

19. a

20. Zoilo Versalles on May 27, 1961, against the Washington Senators

21. Ken Landreaux, 31 games from April 23 to May 30, 1980

22. Lenny Green, 24 games from May 1 to May 28, 1961

23. Rod Carew, .334

24. Kent Hrbek, 23 games from April 17 to May 23, 1982

25. Harmon Killebrew, 1,047

26. Harmon Killebrew, 6,593

27. Harmon Killebrew, 3,412

28. Rod Carew, 1,616

Hitters—Answers

29. Rod Carew, .388 in 1977

30. In 1985 Kirby Puckett had 691 at-bats and 744 plate appearances.

31. Rod Carew, 239 in 1977

32. Randy Bush batted .433 as a pinch-hitter in 1986.

33. Rod Carew had 29 in 1974.

34. He had 16.

35. Zoilo Versalles had 45 in 1965.

36. Tony Oliva had 71 in 1964.

37. Rod Carew led the Twins hitters for nine seasons.

38. Rod Carew led the AL's hitters seven times while with the Twins.

39. Rod Carew was the Twins' top hitter for seven straight seasons (1972-1978).

40. Rod Carew produced 42 four-or-more-hit games during his career with the Twins.

41. Rod Carew (1970), Cesar Tovar (1972), Larry Hisle (1976), Lyman Bostock (1976), Mike Cubbage (1978), Gary Ward (1980) and Kirby Puckett (1986)

42. Rod Carew hit for the cycle on May 20, 1970, against Kansas City in five at-bats.

43. Rod Carew had 12 All-Star Game appearances; Harmon Killebrew was second with 11.

44. Tony Oliva had 28 four-or-more-hit games for the Twins.

45. Tony Oliva led the club six times in batting.

46. Cesar Tovar had two doubles and two home runs against the Angels on May 21, 1967.

47. Rod Carew never played high school baseball but was spotted by scout Herb Klein during play in a New York sandlot league.

48. Rod Carew, five times

Sluggers

1. What Twins player had the most RBIs in one game?

2. What Twins player has hit the most home runs against one team in a single season; who was the team; and in what year?

3. Who are the only Twins players ever to hit three home runs in one game?

4. Where does Tom Brunansky rank in career home runs after the 1987 season?

5. Which Twins player tied a major league record by hitting two home runs on an opening day?

Sluggers—Questions

6. Who is only Twins player ever to hit two inside-the-park homers in one game?

7. What Twins infielder set a fielding mark at first base of .995 and a club grand-slam record of three, both in 1985?

8. What Twins catcher homered in the first two major league games of his career to tie a major league record in 1981?

9. Which Twins right-handed slugger holds the American League record for hitting the most home runs on the road during a single season?

10. What Twins slugger holds the American League lifetime record for home runs by a right-handed hitter?

11. When Roger Maris hit his record-setting 61 home runs during the 1961 season for the Yankees, how many came off Twins pitchers?

12. How many times in his career did Harmon Killebrew hit 40 or more home runs in a single season?

13. Who is the only American League player ever to surpass Harmon Killebrew in hitting 40 or more home runs in one season, and how many times did he do it?

14. What was the best home-run hitting season Kirby Puckett had in the minor leagues?

15. Who is the only Twins player ever to hit a home run in an All-Star Game?

16. Prior to 1987, what was the last Twins team to have three or more players hit 30 or more homers in one season? Name the players and the season.

17. How many times did Harmon Killebrew lead the American League in strikeouts?

18. In 1987 how many Twins players reached double figures in home runs?

19. Who was the first Twins player to hit three home runs in a single game?

20. In 1981 three Twins players hit home runs in their first major league games. Can you name them?

21. Can you name the four Twins players who hit a home run in their first at-bat in the major leagues?

22. In 1965, when the Twins won the American League title, how many home runs and RBIs did Harmon Killebrew accumulate?

23.   Where does Harmon Killebrew rank in lifetime home runs among all major league players?

24.   What player interrupted Harmon Killebrew's string of nine team RBI titles in 11 seasons (1961-1971)?

25.   Which Twins player interrupted Harmon Killebrew's string of 11 home run titles in 12 seasons (1961-1972)?

26.   Who holds the Twins' record for leading the team in consecutive RBI titles, and how many times did he do it?

27.   For how many seasons did Harmon Killebrew lead the Twins in home runs?

28.   How many times did Harmon Killebrew lead the Twins and the American League in home runs, and what were the years?

29.   Who are the Twins players who have led the American League in RBIs during a single season?

30.   Who holds the Twins' record for the most RBIs in a single season, and what was that figure?

31.   What were the most home runs hit in a single season by a Twins player, and who did it?

32. Which player holds the Twins' record for leading the team in home runs over the most consecutive seasons, and what is that number?

33. What players are second to Harmon Killebrew in leading the Twins in RBIs for a single season, and how many times did they do it?

34. Which players are second to Harmon Killebrew in leading the Twins in home runs, and how many seasons did they lead the team?

35. In 1969 Harmon Killebrew drew five more bases on balls than he had RBIs. How many of each did he have?

36. Which Twins player holds the record for most home runs in opposing parks during a single season and he also holds the record for the most at home?

37. Who holds the record for hitting home runs in consecutive games, and how many games were involved?

38. Which Twins players hold the season record for grand slams?

39. Who was the rookie hitter who not only led the Twins but also set an American

League record for most homers in one season (until Mark McGwire's total in 1987)?

40. Which Twins player holds the record for most home runs by a left-handed hitter in a single season?

41. Who holds the single-season all-time slugging percentage, and what is the mark?

42. Which player holds the Twins' season record for most extra-base hits?

43. Which Twins player is just one of six major leaguers who have hit 20 or more homers for the past six seasons?

44. What Twins players have hit the most inside-the-park home runs?

45. Who was the first Twins player to hit an inside-the-park home run?

46. Harmon Killebrew holds the Twins' all-time RBI lead with:
     a) 1,462
     b) 1,325
     c) 1,380
     d) 1,292

47. Who were the six Twins players to hit 20 or more home runs in 1964, and how many did each have?

48. Who is the only Twins player ever to hit a pinch-hit inside-the-park homer, and when did he do it?

49. Which Twins player holds the club record for pinch-hit grand-slam homers?

50. Who is the only Twins pitcher ever to hit a grand-slam home run?

51. Harmon Killebrew is the Twins all-time grand-slam home run leader with:
    a) 14
    b) 11
    c) 13
    d) 10

52. Who hit the first grand-slam home run in Twins history; in what inning; and against what team?

53. In what season did the Twins tie a major league record for most home runs, and what was the mark?

54. How many home runs did the Twins hit in a game against the Washington Senators in 1963 to tie a major league team record?

55. Who is the only Twins player ever to hit two inside-the-park home runs in one game?

56.　　Harmon Killebrew is the team's all-time home run leader. How many did he hit while playing for the Twins?
   a) 506
   b) 475
   c) 490
   d) 432

Answers

1. Glen Adams knocked in eight runs against the White Sox on June 26, 1977.

2. Harmon Killebrew hit 11 home runs against the Oakland A's in 1969.

3. Bob Allison, Harmon Killebrew and Tony Oliva

4. Brunansky is fourth on the Twins' all-time list with 162 and first among all active players.

5. Gary Gaetti hit two homers on opening day 1982 to tie the major league mark.

6. Greg Gagne hit two inside-the-park

homers off Toronto's Jim Clancy in 1986, the only Twin to perform such a feat.

7. Kent Hrbek set both a fielding record and a grand-slam mark the same season.

8. Tim Laudner, on August 27-28, 1981

9. Harmon Killebrew hit 28 homers on the road during the 1962 season.

10. Harmon Killebrew's 573 homers are the most by a right-handed hitter in AL history.

11. Twins pitchers gave up four of Maris's 61 homers, two by Pete Ramos and one by Camilo Pascual and Ed Palmquist.

12. Killebrew had seven seasons as a Twins player in which he hit 40 or more homers.

13. Babe Ruth hit 40 or more in the American League 11 times; Killebrew did it eight times.

14. Puckett hit nine home runs for Visalia in 1983.

15. Harmon Killebrew hit three homers in All-Star competition, the only ones by any Twins player.

16. In 1964 Harmon Killebrew (49), Bob Allison (32) and Tony Oliva (32) were on the last Twins team where three hitters had 30 or more home runs.

17. Just once

18. Eight Twins hit 10 or more homers in 1987, the fourth time in the team's history such a record has been tied.

19. Bob Allison had three homers at Cleveland on May 17, 1963.

20. Kent Hrbek, Tim Laudner and Gary Gaetti all hit homers in their first Twins games in the majors.

21. Rick Renick, Dave McKay, Gary Gaetti and Andre David all hit home runs in their first major league at-bat for the Twins.

22. Killebrew hit 25 homers and drove in 75 runs for the AL champion Twins.

23. Killebrew ranks fifth in home runs with a lifetime number of 573.

24. Tony Oliva broke a four-year run in 1965 with 98 RBIs, and again in 1968 with 68.

25. Bob Allison led the 1968 team with 22 home runs.

26. Harmon Killebrew was the Twins' top RBI leader in four straight seasons (1961-1964).

27. Killebrew led the Twins in homers for 11 seasons.

28. Killebrew led the team and the AL four times (48-1962; 45-1963; 49-1964; 49-1969).

29. Harmon Killebrew was the AL's RBI leader in 1962 (126); 1969 (140); 1971 (119); and Larry Hisle in 1977 (119).

30. Harmon Killebrew drove in 140 runs during the 1969 season.

31. Harmon Killebrew twice hit 49, in 1964 and 1969.

32. Harmon Killebrew led the team for seven straight seasons (1961-1967).

33. Tony Oliva and Kent Hrbek each did it three times.

34. Roy Smalley led the Twins three times (19-1978; 24-1980; 7-1981); and Tom Brunansky has led three times (28-1983; 32-1984; 27-1985).

35. Killebrew walked 145 times, but he drove in 140 runs.

36. Harmon Killebrew hit 28 in 1962 and 29 at the Met in 1961.

37. Harmon Killebrew hit a home run in five straight games during the 1970 season.

38. Three each by Bob Allison (1961), Rod Carew (1976) and Kent Hrbek (1985)

39. Jimmie Hall hit 33 in 1963.

40. Ken Hrbek hit 34 in 1987 to break Jimmie Hall's old mark of 33.

41. Harmon Killebrew had a slugging mark of .606 in 1961.

42. Tony Oliva had 84 in 1964.

43. Tom Brunansky

44. Tony Oliva and Tom Brunansky each have hit three.

45. Harmon Killebrew, July 4, 1961

46. b

47. Harmon Killebrew (49), Jimmy Hall (25), Bob Allison (32), Don Mincher (23), Tony Oliva (32) and Zoilo Versalles (20)

48. Tom Brunansky, on July 19, 1982, against Milwaukee

Sluggers—Answers

49. Rich Reese with three

50. Camilo Pascual, on April 27, 1965, against the Cleveland Indians

51. d

52. Bob Allison in the first inning of a game against Baltimore on April 16, 1961

53. In May 1964, the Twins tied the New York Giants' mark of 55 homers in one month.

54. The Twins pounded eight home runs against the Senators on August 29, 1963.

55. Greg Gagne, on October 4, 1986

56. b

Pitchers

1. Who is the all-time winningest Twins pitcher?

2. Who lead the Twins in saves in 1987, and how many did he have?

3. Which Twins pitcher became the 25th teenager ever to win ten games in a major league season?

4. Of Bert Blyleven's three career one-hitters, how many were pitched at home for the Twins?

5. Which Twins pitcher hurled the most innings in a single game, and against whom?

6. Name the four Twins pitchers who have accumulated club-leading 15 strikeouts in one game.

7. Which Twins pitcher holds the record for consecutive strikeouts, how many did he have, and against whom?

8. What are the most home runs given up by Bert Blyleven in one game, and against which team?

9. Who is the only Twins pitcher ever to hit three batters in each of three different games?

10. Who is the only major league relief pitcher to have 20 or more saves for the last five seasons?

11. Which Twins pitcher won the most consecutive games in one season?

12. Who is the Twins' all-time leader for receiving the Joseph W. Haynes award, given each year to the top pitcher?

13. Who pitched the first no-hitter in Twins history, and who did he beat?

14. What Twins pitcher had the distinction of hurling two no-hitters in the same season, and what was the year?

15. What teams did he beat?

16. Who is the only Twins pitcher to be given credit for a perfect game and why does it carry an asterisk?

17. What Twins pitcher holds the best all-time won-lost percentage?

18. Which Twins pitcher has the best single-season won-lost percentage?

19. Which Twins pitcher holds the career club record for pitching the most innings?

20. Who was the Twins pitcher who tied Mike Cuellar of Baltimore for most victories in the major leagues in 1970, and how many did he have?

21. Who are the only two Twins pitchers ever to lead the American League outright in wins for a season, how many and when?

22. Which Twins pitcher had the fewest wins in leading the club, and how many did he have?

23. Who is the only native Minnesotan ever to lead the Twins in pitching victories, how many times and in what seasons?

24. Which Twins pitcher has led the club in victories the most times, and how often did he do it?

25. Who was the Twins' first 20-game winner?

26. Which Twins pitcher led the team in victories in their first season and how many did he win?

27. What Twins pitcher won the most games during a single season?

28. Who is the Twins' all-time winningest right-handed pitcher and how many games did he win?

29. Who holds the Twins' record for winning the most consecutive games?

30. Which Twins pitcher is credited with the lowest career earned run mark?

31. Which pitcher led the Twins for the most seasons with the lowest earned run average?

32. Which pitcher was the team's earned run leader in the Twins first season?

33. What Twins pitcher had the best single-season earned run average?

34. Which Twins pitcher has won the most opening games, either home or away, in team history?

35. Which Twins pitcher has won the most home openers in team history?

36. In 1973 this Twins pitcher established club season records for both innings pitched and hits allowed. Who was it and what were his numbers?

37. Which Twins right-hander has pitched the most shutouts in the team's history?

38. Which pitcher has hurled the most shutouts as a Twins player?

39. Which Twins pitcher has recorded the most shutouts during a single season?

40. Which Twins pitcher has recorded the most consecutive shut-out innings during a regular season?

41. Which pitcher in Twins history has won the most 1-0 games in a single season?

42. Which Twins pitcher has hurled the most shutouts?

43. Who is the only Twins pitcher ever to lead the American League in strikeouts; how many times and in what seasons did he do it?

44. How many times has Bert Blyleven led the Twins in strikeouts?

45. In 1973, the same season in which he set club marks for innings pitched and hits allowed, Bert Blyleven also established a mark of how many strikeouts?

46. Who is the Twins' all-time strikeout leader?

47. What is the record this Twins pitcher holds for completing the most games in 1973?

48. What Twins pitcher holds the single season record for starting the most games? What is the record?

49. What is the record for most consecutive complete games by a Twins pitcher in a season, and who set it?

50. Which Twins pitcher is credited with the most complete games in team history?

51. Which Twins pitcher has appeared in the most games in club history?

52. Which Twins pitcher has started the most games in Twins history?

53. Which Twins pitcher has been charged with the most losses?

54. What Twins pitcher issued the most walks during a single season, and what was the figure?

55. What pitcher issued the most intentional walks in a single Twins season, and how many did he issue?

56. Which Twins relief pitcher is credited with the most saves?

57. Who is the all-time single-season saves leader among Twins relief pitchers?

58. Which Twins relief pitcher won the most games during one season?

59. This Twins relief pitcher established both a club and league record for appearances in a single season. Who was he and in how many games did he appear?

60. Mike Marshall's record-setting 90 appearances included how many relief jobs during 1979?

61. This Twins pitcher established a major league, as well as a club single season record, by finishing how many games in 1979?

62. What relief pitcher appeared in 281 games over five seasons for the Twins and saved 69 of them?

63. One Twins pitcher holds the team record for consecutive losing games, and for consecutive losses in one season. Who is he?

64. Who is the Twins' single-season leader in the fine art of picking runners off base?

65. What is the Twins' single-season record for most balks by a pitcher, and who holds it?

66. In 1976 this pitcher set a club record for wild pitches. Who was it, and how many did he throw?

67. Who holds the single-season record for most hit batsman among all Twins pitchers, and how many did he hit?

68. Which pitcher holds the dubious distinction of surrendering the most home runs in club history?

69. Which Twins pitcher has given up the most hits in team history?

70. Who is the only Twins pitcher to win the Cy Young award in the American League?

71. This Twins pitcher was the acknowledged "gopher ball' champion of baseball in 1986 with how many record-setting HRs allowed?

Answers

1. Jim Kaat, 189 victories

2. Jeff Reardon had 31.

3. Bert Blyleven was still a teenager when he won 10 games for the Twins in 1970.

4. Two of his one-hitters came in the Twin Cities, against Kansas City in 1973 and in 1974 over Texas.

5. Jim Merritt pitched 13 innings against the Yankees on July 26, 1967.

6. Camilo Pascual, Joe Decker, Jerry Koosman and Bert Blyleven

7.   Jim Merritt struck out seven straight Washington batters on July 21, 1966.

8.   Blyleven surrendered five against the Texas Rangers on September 13, 1986.

9.   Jim Kaat hit three batters working against Chicago (1961), Cleveland (1962) and New York (1962).

10.   The Twins' Jeff Reardon

11.   Stan Williams won nine straight in 1970.

12.   Bert Blyleven, three times (1971, 1973, 1986)

13.   Jack Kralick, 1-0 against the Kansas City A's, 1962

14.   Dean Chance, 1967

15.   Boston and Cleveland

16.   Dean Chance who beat the Red Sox 2-0 on August 8, 1967, in a rain-shortened game

17.   Camilo Pascual, .607 (88-57)

18.   Bill Campbell posted a .773 mark in 1976 on his 17-5 record for pitchers with 10 or more decisions.

19.   Jim Kaat, 2,958

20.   Jim Perry won 24 games in 1970 to tie Cuellar.

21.   Jim (Mudcat) Grant had 21 in 1965 and Jim Kaat had 25 in 1966.

22.   Pete Redfern's nine wins in 1981, the strike season, topped the Twins.

23.   Jerry Koosman won 20 games in 1977 and 16 games in 1978.

24.   Bert Blyleven has led the club in wins four times.

25.   Camilo Pascual had a 20-11 record in 1962.

26.   Camilo Pascual, with 15 wins in 1961

27.   Jim Kaat won 25 games in 1966.

28.   Bert Blyleven has won 139 games.

29.   Bert Blyleven and Ray Corbin each won 10 in a row, Blyleven in 1971-1972 and Corbin in 1973-1974.

30.   Al Worthington, 2.62

31.   Bert Blyleven has led the team with the lowest season ERA five times.

Pitchers—Answers

32. Camilo Pascual, with a 3.46 mark

33. Camilo Pascual had a 2.47 ERA over 248 innings in 1963.

34. Jim Perry

35. Bert Blyleven, three

36. Bert Blyleven pitched 325 innings and allowed 296 hits.

37. Camilo Pascual, 18

38. Bert Blyleven has 29 career shutouts with the Twins.

39. Bert Blyleven did it nine times in 1973.

40. Jim Kaat with 29⅔ in 1966

41. Bert Blyleven won three 1-0 games in 1971.

42. Bert Blyleven has 55, but 26 of those have come with other major league teams.

43. Camilo Pascual did it in 1961, 1962 and 1963.

44. Blyleven has been the club strikeout leader six times, more than any pitcher in team history.

45.   He struck out 258 batters.

46.   Jim Kaat

47.   Bert Blyleven finished 25 of his starts in 1973.

48.   Jim Kaat started 42 games in 1965 en route to helping the Twins to the AL pennant.

49.   Camilo Pascual completed eight straight games in 1964.

50.   Jim Kaat, 133

51.   Jim Kaat, 468

52.   Jim Kaat, 422

53.   Jim Kaat, 152

54.   Jim Hughes walked 127 in 1975.

55.   Ron Perranoski walked 16 batters intentionally in 1969.

56.   Ron Davis, 108

57.   Ron Perranoski saved 34 games in 1970.

58.   Bill Campbell won 17 in 1976.

59.   Mike Marshall appeared in 90 games in 1979.

60.   Eighty-nine of those games were in relief.

61.   Mike Marshall finished 84 of his 90 appearances that year.

62.   Al Worthington

63.   Terry Felton lost 16 straight between 1980 and 1982; 13 of those came in 1982.

64.   Jerry Koosman did it 14 times in 1979.

65.   Roger Erickson was charged with five balks in 1981.

66.   Dave Goltz was charged with 15, a record tied in 1986 by Mike Smithson.

67.   Jim Kaat hit 18 batters in 1962.

68.   Jim Kaat, 270

69.   Jim Kaat, 2,927

70.   Jim Perry, 1970

71.   Bert Blyleven allowed 50 home runs.

Twin Cities

1.   What was the trade that brought outfielder Tom Brunansky to the Twins?

2.   What is Frank Viola's status among the major league's left-handed pitchers over the last four seasons (1984-1987)?

3.   What was the outcome of the Twins' American League divisional playoffs against the Baltimore Orioles in 1969 and 1970?

4.   What school did Gary Gaetti attend, and in what round was he picked by the Twins?

5.   What is the Twins' all-time team winning streak, and in what season did it occur?

6.   Where was Kent Hrbek picked by the Twins in the 1978 draft?

7.   Who was the Twins' winning pitcher in the first game the club ever played, and who did he beat?

8.   What was the date on which the Twins played their first game in the Twin Cities, and what was the result?

9.   On what date did Twins owner Carl Pohlad purchase the Twins from Calvin Griffith and his sister?

10.   Who was the first Twins manager?

11.   What was Billy Martin's record during his single season as Twins manager?

12.   Which Twins player led the team in RBIs during the 1961 season and how many did he have?

13.   Can you name the pitching staff for the 1961 Twins?

14.   Who succeeded Cookie Lavagetto as Twins manager during the 1961 season and eventually led the team into the 1965 World Series?

15.   Which Twins manager had the best single-season record?

16. Which Twins manager has won the most games?

17. Can you name the Twins' outfielders on their first 1961 original roster?

18. Can you name the infielders on the Twins' original 1961 roster?

19. Who were the three catchers on the Twins' original 1961 roster?

20. Which Twins hitter led the team in home runs in its first 1961 season and how many did he have?

21. Which player led the Twins in hitting during its first season (1961)?

22. What Twins player set an American League stolen base record in the first half of the 1968 season, and what was the record?

23. What Twins player became the first American Leaguer ever to play all nine positions in one game?

24. Who was the Twins first baseman who won seven Gold Glove awards during his major league career, including three seasons with the Twins?

25.   Name the two Oakland A's pitchers who hurled no-hitters against the Twins.

26.   Which Twins infielder holds the All-Star Game record for most putouts in an extra-inning game?

27.   Which Twins infielder shares an All-Star Game record for participating in the most double plays?

28.   Do you recall the momentous trade between the Indians and Twins that brought Luis Tiant to Minnesota?

29.   Can you recall the principals in the blockbuster trade that sent Mudcat Grant to the Dodgers before the 1968 season?

30.   Graig Nettles finished his 21st year of major league baseball in 1987, but do you recall his first major league hit for the Twins in 1967?

31.   Which Twins player won AL Comeback of the Year honors in 1967?

32.   This former Twins outfielder also played fullback for the University of Kansas. Who was he?

33.   What was Sam Mele's job with the Twins before he was picked to succeed Cookie Lavagetto as manager in 1961?

34. Where did the Twins finish in 1964, the year before they won the AL title, and what was their record?

35. How did the Twins finish in 1966, the year after they won the AL pennant?

36. Who replaced Twins manager Sam Mele during the 1967 season?

37. Who were the four catchers used by the Twins in a 1967 game against the Angels that tied an American League record?

38. Do you remember the unusual nicknames of former Twins Bob Allison and Jim Merritt?

39. How many times in its history has the Metrodome roof collapsed under the weight of a winter's snow?

40. Which Twins team compiled the best home record, and within three, how many did it win?

41. How many pitchers who have accumulated 2,000 or more strikeouts have pitched for the Twins during their career?

42. What was the uniform number of Rod Carew which was retired during the 1987 season?

43. In 1982 how many rookies were on the Twins' 24-man roster at the end of the season?

44. Who were the veteran players traded by Calvin Griffith during the 1982 season?

45. Whom did the Twins receive from the White Sox when they traded Roy Smalley in 1984?

46. Whom did the Twins receive from Texas when they traded Bert Blyleven in 1976?

47. Whom did the Twins give up to get Roy Smalley back from the White Sox?

48. How many knuckleball pitchers have worked for the Twins?

49. Which Twins player won the All-Star Game's "Slugger's Contest" in 1985?

50. Whom did the Twins trade to the Indians in 1985 to reclaim pitcher Bert Blyleven?

51. Who were the Oakland A's players who hit three consecutive home runs off Jim Kaat in a 1963 game?

52. The Metrodome once was the scene of three consecutive home runs by Detroit's Kirk Gibson, Lance Parrish and Darrell Evans off which Twins pitcher?

53. Who was the first Twins player ever to hit a home run in his first major league at-bat?

54. Who comprised the Twins' first broadcasting team in 1961?

55. Ironically, in 1965, when the Twins won their first AL title, they also had the smallest crowd in their history. How many, within 100 persons, showed up to watch a game against Kansas City?

56. What was the largest crowd ever to see the Twins play, and where was the site?

57. Which player in Twins history has had the longest last name?

58. Can you name the two Twins players who have had the shortest last names?

59. Who turned the Twins' first triple play, and against which team?

60. How many triple plays have the Twins produced?

61. Which Twins players have been involved in the most triple plays?

62. Which major league player got the first hit in the Metrodome, and when?

63. Which Twins player had the first official hit in the Metrodome?

64. What was the largest crowd ever to see the Twins play at Metropolitan Stadium?

65. Which Twins player holds the record for the longest hitless streak?

66. Which Twins player has won the most Gold Glove awards?

67. Which Twins player hit the first home run at Metropolitan Stadium?

68. Which Twins player hit the last home run at Metropolitan Stadium?

69. Under what circumstance, against whom and when did the weather cause a game at the Metrodome to be postponed?

70. Which player had the first hit in the history of the Twins franchise?

71. Can you name the three Twins pitchers who have gone to bat since the designated hitter rule was established, and what they did?

72. What was the first major league team to select Gary Gaetti in the draft?

73. Who was the Twins scout who signed Frank Viola and former Twins star Rod Carew?

74. How many minor league games did Frank Viola pitch in the Twins organization before joining the team in 1982?

75. In what round, and in what year was Frank Viola picked by the Twins?

76. What Twins pitcher, before the DH, was credited with the most sacrifice hits in a game?

77. What Twins player holds the record for the most stolen bases in one game?

78. Who was the Twins' starting pitcher on the final day of the 1967 season when they played the Red Sox with a chance to win the American League title?

79. Who is the only player ever to hit a pair of inside-the-park home runs against the Twins, and who was the pitcher?

80. When the Twins played in the first American League playoff game under the split league set-up, who were the starting and losing pitchers?

81. Game situation: 12th inning of first AL playoff in 1969, the Orioles' Mark

Belanger on third, two out. What happened next?

82. How did the Twins lose the second game of the 1969 AL playoffs to the Orioles?

83. How did Orioles manager Earl Weaver deal with Harmon Killebrew during the 1969 AL playoff series?

84. Do you remember the distances to left, center and right fields at Metropolitan Stadium?

85. How many times have the Twins finished with a .500 or better record?

86. What team did the Twins beat out for the AL-West title in 1970?

87. Who managed the Twins to their 1970 AL-West championship?

88. What was the outcome of the first game ever played at the Metrodome?

89. What were the preseason odds on the Twins winning the 1987 American League pennant, and the odds on them taking the World Series?

Answers

1. In 1982 the Twins traded pitcher Doug Corbett and infielder Rob Wilfong for Brunansky and pitcher Mike Walters.

2. He has the most victories, 69.

3. They lost each year, 3 games to 0.

4. Gaetti played at Northwest Missouri State and he was a first-round pick in June, 1978.

5. Twelve in 1980 against Chicago, Texas and Kansas City

6. Number 17

7.   Pete Ramos defeated Whitey Ford of the Yankees, 6-0, on April 11, 1961, at Yankee Stadium.

8.   On April 21, 1961, the Twins were defeated by the Washington Senators, 5-3, before 24,606 at Metropolitan Stadium.

9.   September 7, 1984

10.   Cookie Lavagetto

11.   97-65 in 1969

12.   Harmon Killebrew drove in 122 runs to lead the 1961 team.

13.   Fred Bruckbauer, Paul Giel, Jim Kaat, Jack Kralick, Don Lee, Ray Moore, Camilo Pascual, Bill Pleis, Pete Ramos, Ted Sadowski, Lee Stange and Chuck Stobbs

14.   Sam Mele

15.   Sam Mele, 102-60 in 1965

16.   Sam Mele, 522

17.   Bob Allison, Don Dobbek, Lenny Green, Jim Lemon, Elmer Valo and Pete Whisenant

18. Reno Bertoia, Billy Consolo, Billy Gardner, Harmon Killebrew, Don Mincher, Jose Valdivielso and Zoilo Versalles

19. Earl Battey, Hal Naragon and Ron Henry

20. Harmon Killebrew hit 46 to lead the 1961 Twins.

21. Earl Battey hit .302 as the team's number-one catcher.

22. Rod Carew stole home seven times.

23. Cesar Tovar played all nine positions on September 22, 1968.

24. Vic Power

25. Jim (Catfish) Hunter and Vida Blue

26. Harmon Killebrew recorded 15 in the 1967 All-Star game that went 15 innings.

27. Harmon Killebrew participated in six double plays as a fielder, sharing an All-Star Game mark with Bill White of the National League.

28. The Twins traded Graig Nettles, pitchers Dean Chance and Bob Miller, and outfielder Ted Uhlaender to the Indians for pitchers Luis Tiant and Stan Williams in 1969.

29. The Twins traded Grant and Zoilo Versalles to the Dodgers for catcher John Roseboro and pitchers Bob Miller and Ron Perranoski.

30. Nettles doubled for his only hit in three at-bats late in the 1967 season.

31. Pitcher Dean Chance was picked as AL Comeback Player of the Year in 1967 after a 20-14 season following a 12-17 mark in 1966 with the Angels.

32. Bob Allison played fullback for Kansas before signing a pro baseball contract.

33. Mele was the Twins' third base coach.

34. The Twins finished sixth, with a 79-83 record.

35. The Twins finished second in the American League, beating Baltimore on the last day of the season to secure that spot.

36. Cal Ermer was picked as manager during the 1967 season.

37. The Twins used catchers Jerry Zimmerman, Russ Nixon, Hank Izquierdo and Earl Battey in one game, tying an AL mark.

38. Allison's nickname with the Twins was "Bubble Up" and Merritt's was "Bones."

39. Four . . . . so far!

40. The 1969 team won 57 games at home, one more than the 1987 team.

41. Six pitchers who have 2,000 or more strikeouts have been Twins pitchers— Steve Carlton, Bert Blyleven, Jim Kaat, Luis Tiant, Jerry Koosman and Camilo Pascual.

42. Carew wore number 29.

43. The Twins had 15 rookies on their roster for most of the 1982 season.

44. Griffith traded Doug Corbett, Rob Wilfong, Butch Wynegar and Roy Smalley.

45. The Twins received pitchers Doug Drabel and Kevin Hickey for Smalley.

46. The Twins got pitcher Bill Singer, infielders Roy Smalley, Mike Cubbage, pitcher Jim Gideon and $250,000 for Blyleven and infielder Danny Thompson.

47. The Twins sent first baseman Randy Johnson and outfielder Ron Scheer to the White Sox for Smalley.

48. Only one, Joe Niekro, who was obtained midway through the 1987 season

49. Tom Brunansky beat all of major league home run hitters to win the slugger's contest.

50. The Twins sent pitchers Curt Wardle, and Rich Yett, minor leaguer infielder Jay Bell and outfielder Jim Weaver.

51. Ted Kubiak, Reggie Jackson and Sal Bando

52. Bert Blyleven gave up those homers in the fourth inning of a Tigers 5-1 win.

53. Rick Renick hit a 3-1 pitch by Detroit pitcher Mickey Lolich for a homer on July 11, 1968, in his first major league at-bat.

54. Ray Scott, Bob Wolff and Halsey Hall made up the Twins first broadcasting team.

55. 537 persons saw the Twins-A's on September 20, 1965.

56. A crowd of 71,245 showed up at Yankee Stadium on June 20, 1965, to watch the Twins.

57. Pitcher Paul Thormodsgard, all 12 letters in the last name

58.   Pitcher Don Lee (1961-1962) and infielder Joe Lis (1973-1974)

59.   Rich Rollins, Cesar Tovar and Harmon Killebrew turned a grounder by the Red Sox Frank Malzone into a triple play on August 18, 1966.

60.   The Twins have turned six triple plays.

61.   Gary Gaetti and Kent Hrbek each have been involved in three triple plays for the Twins.

62.   Pete Rose of the Phillies hit a single to center in the first inning of an April 3, 1982, exhibition game.

63.   Dave Engle of the Twins hit a home run against Seattle in the first inning of the April 6, 1962, season opener.

64.   A crowd of 50,596 watched the Twins and Dodgers in the seventh game of the World Series in 1965.

65.   In the pre-DH days, pitcher Dean Chance went 53 straight at-bats without a hit.

66.   Pitcher Jim Kaat won 11 straight Gold Glove awards.

67.   Don Mincher hit the first home run off

Washington's Joe McClain in the fourth inning of the first game.

68. Pete Mackanin hit the final homer for the Twins at the Met on September 30, 1981.

69. A snowstorm prevented a flight carrying the California Angels from landing in the Twin Cities, causing the April 14 game to be postponed.

70. Harmon Killebrew singled off the Yankees' Whitey Ford in the fourth inning at Yankee Stadium on April 11, 1961.

71. Vic Albury and Bill Campbell each batted against the Yankees on July 12, 1975, and struck out. So did Ray Fontenot in 1986.

72. The St. Louis Cardinals, in 1978

73. Rod Stein

74. Twenty-five (17 at Orlando, 8 at Toledo)

75. He was a second-round draft pick in June, 1981.

76. Bert Blyleven had three sacrifices against the Orioles on July 27, 1970.

77. Larry Hisle stole four bases against the Royals on June 30, 1976.

78. Dean Chance started the last game of the 1967 season against the Red Sox.

79. Rich Allen of the White Sox hit a pair of inside-the-park HRs against Bert Blyleven on July 31, 1972.

80. Jim Perry started for the Twins but reliever Ron Perranoski lost a 4-3, 12-inning decision on October 4, 1969.

81. Paul Blair acted on his own and laid down a perfect squeeze bunt that drove in the tie-breaking run.

82. Curt Motton hit a two-out pinch single off reliever Ron Perranoski that scored Boog Powell from second base for a 1-0, 11-inning victory.

83. Deathly afraid of Killebrew's power, Weaver had him walked five times in the first two games, giving him just five official at-bats.

84. It was 346 feet to left, 425 feet to center and 330 feet to right field in the Met.

85. The Twins have been .500 or better 15 times since 1961.

86. The Twins finished nine games ahead of the Oakland A's when they won the 1970 AL-West title.

87.   Bill Rigney was the Twins manager in 1970.

88.   Seattle defeated the Twins, 11-7, in that first game.

89.   75 to 1 to win the AL; 150 to 1 to win the World Series

The 1965 Season

1. When the Twins hosted the All-Star game in 1965, who were its representatives on the AL squad?

2. Whose home run tied the score, 5-5, in the fifth inning of the 1965 All-Star game?

3. How much did each Twins player earn for a full World Series share in 1965?

4. A solid indication of the respect that opposing pitchers gave Twins hitters on the 1965 team was the number of intentional walks issued. How many were there?

5. The 1965 team was renowned for its power, but what was the team-record

number of fewest double plays that opponents recorded?

6. The 1965 team set a team record by producing how many sacrifice flies?

7. One of the hallmarks of the 1965 team was its ability to win doubleheaders. How many?

8. The 1965 team was the toughest in Twins history to shut out. It was held scoreless how many times?

9. The Twins' jack-rabbit baserunners produced a team record for success in stolen base attempts in 1965. It was:
   a) .659
   b) .700
   c) .736
   d) .593

10. Who led the team in hitting during the Twins' 1965 AL title season, and what did he hit?

11. Which player led the Twins in RBIs that year and how many did he drive in?

12. Who was the Twins' leading home run hitter during its 1965 AL championship season, and how many did he have?

13. Which American League team was the perfect patsy for the Twins during their 1965 AL title season?

14. Name the pitcher who had the pennant clinching victory in 1965 for the Twins. Who did he beat?

15. How many home runs did the Twins hit during the 1965 season, and who was the leader?

16. Who were the Twins' leading hitters in the 1965 World Series?

17. What was the crucial play made by the Dodgers' Jim Gilliam in the fifth inning of the seventh game of the 1965 Series that ended the Twins' only serious scoring threat?

18. Who was the American League 1965 Manager of the Year?

19. How many hits did Koufax allow in the seventh game of the 1965 Series, and how many Twins did he strike out?

20. Who was the Twins' starter and loser in Game 7 of the 1965 Series?

21. Who drove in the Dodgers' runs in the 1965 seventh series game, and how did they happen?

22. What was the final score of the seventh game of the 1965 World Series?

23. Who was the only pitcher to hit a home run in the 1965 Series?

24. On how many days rest did Sandy Koufax pitch against the Twins in the seventh game of the 1965 World Series?

25. Who was the only member of the Twins 1965 team to have faced Sandy Koufax in his very first major league start?

26. True or false: When the Twins played the Dodgers in the 1965 World Series, it was the first time they ever played in Dodgers Stadium.

27. Which Twins pitcher got the Series tied 3-3 at MetropolitanStadium; who did he beat; and what was the score?

28. Who were the Twins pitchers who were the victims of Dodgers shutouts in Los Angeles during the 1965 World Series, and who beat them?

29. Which Twins outfielder made what is now considered one of the greatest catches in World Series history when he caught Jim Lefebvre's curving liner with a man on base?

30. Who was the Twins' winning pitcher in Game 2 of the 1965 World Series; who did he beat; and what was the score?

31. Whose three-run homer in the third inning of the first game keyed a six-run rally and led the Twins to victory?

32. Which Twins pitcher was the winner of Game 1 of the 1965 World Series; who did he beat; and what was the score?

33. What was the nature of Harmon Killebrew's injury that cost him 48 games during the Twins' 1965 pennant-winning year?

34. Who was third base coach for the Twins in their 1965 pennant season?

35. In what games did Sandy Koufax beat the Twins in the 1965 World Series?

36. In the 1965 World Series, Dodgers pitcher Sandy Koufax declined to pitch the first game for what reason?

37. Which Twins player led the American League in batting, total hits and tied for first in sacrifice flies with 10?

38. Which Twins player was named American League Player of the Year in 1965?

39. Who was the former Dodgers clubhouse boy in LA who pitched in two games against them for the Twins in the 1965 Series?

40. Who were the Dodgers' relief pitchers in the 1965 Series who three years later wound up pitching for the Twins?

41. Who was the second baseman recalled from the Twins' Denver farm midway through the 1965 season who helped stabilize the team's infield en route to the AL title?

42. This Twins third baseman in 1965 had the unusual distinction of playing for both the American and National League All Star teams in one season. Who was he?

43. Can you name two significant events surrounding the 1965 All-Star Game, the Twins and the Twin Cities?

44. Which American League team did the Twins beat out for their 1965 AL title?

45. Who was the MVP in the 1965 World Series between the Twins and Dodgers?

Answers

1. Manager Sam Mele, catcher Earl Battey, pitcher Jim Kaat (replaced by Mudcat Grant), first baseman Harmon Killebrew, and outfielder Tony Oliva represented the Twins at the 1965 All-Star Game.

2. Harmon Killebrew of the Twins hit a two-run homer, the second of the inning, to tie the score.

3. $6,634

4. A team record 79 intentional bases on balls were given Twins hitters in 1965.

5. That year the Twins team hit into only 93 double plays.

The 1965 Season—Answers

6. Twins hitters had 59 sacrifice flies in 1965.

7. The 1965 team won a team-record seven doubleheaders.

8. It suffered only three shutouts.

9. c) The Twins stole 92 bases, got caught just 33 times for a .736 percentage.

10. Tony Oliva led the Twins with a league-leading .321 average.

11. Tony Oliva drove in 98 runs to lead the Twins.

12. Harmon Killebrew hit 25 homers to lead the Twins that year.

13. The Twins had a 17-1 series edge over the Boston Red Sox.

14. Jim Kaat defeated the Washington Senators.

15. The Twins hit 150 homers in 1965, led by Harmon Killebrew's 25.

16. Harmon Killebrew and Zoilo Versalles each batted .286.

17. Gilliam dove to his right to grab Zoilo Versalles's grounder with runners on second

and first, and stepped on third for the final out of the inning.

18. Sam Mele of the Twins

19. Koufax allowed just three hits and struck out 10 batters.

20. Jim Kaat started and allowed both runs before being lifted in the fourth inning.

21. Lou Johnson hit a solo home run and Wes Parker singled home Ron Fairly in the fourth inning.

22. The Dodgers beat the Twins, 2-0.

23. Jim Mudcat Grant

24. Koufax pitched with only two days' rest.

25. Manager Sam Mele batted against Koufax at Ebbets Field in his first start, and hit a double.

26. False. The California Angels also played there in 1965 while their new park in Anaheim was under construction.

27. Mudcat Grant beat the Dodgers, 5-1.

28. Claude Osteen beat Camilo Pascual, 4-0, and Sandy Koufax beat Jim Kaat, 7-0.

29.   Twins left-fielder Bob Allison made the catch and slid about 15 feet along the outfield after securing the ball.

30.   Jim Kaat defeated Sandy Koufax, 5-1.

31.   Zoilo Versalles hit a three-run homer off Drysdale in the third for a 4-1 Twins lead, and they added three more.

32.   Mudcat Grant defeated Don Drysdale, 8-2.

33.   Killebrew dislocated his elbow.

34.   Billy Martin

35.   Koufax won Games 5 and 7.

36.   Because he was Jewish, he deferred to the holiday, Yom Kippur.

37.   Tony Oliva batted .321 and had 185 hits to lead the American League in 1965.

38.   Tony Oliva

39.   Jim Merritt was a clubhouse boy for the Dodgers when they occupied the LA Coliseum in the late sixties, then signed with the Twins organization in 1962.

40.   Bob Miller and Ron Perranoski each pitched two games for the Dodgers in the

1965 Series and were traded to the Twins before the 1968 season.

41.   Frank Quilici

42.   Rich Rollins played for the Senators and the Cubs when picked to the AL and NL All-Star teams in 1962, when the game was played twice that season.

43.   Ironically, the 1965 game was played at Metropolitan Stadium, later the site for the World Series, and the NL's 6-5 lead gave them a series lead for good.

44.   The Twins finished seven games ahead of the Chicago White Sox for the 1965 AL pennant.

45.   Sandy Koufax

1987 Season and Playoffs

1. What was the earned run mark of pitcher Frank Viola in 1987, and where did it place him among AL pitchers?

2. Name the Twins players who have played in the NCAA's College World Series.

3. Who were the only rookies to make the Twins' 24-man roster at the end of spring training in 1987?

4. Against what team did Jeff Reardon get his first save for the Twins in 1987?

5. Kirby Puckett is tops among current Twins players with homers in how many consecutive games?

6.   What team did Les Straker defeat in 1987 for his first major league win?

7.   At what spot in the hitting order did Puckett bat before being moved when Tom Kelly became Twins manager?

8.   Can you detail the baseball lineage of Twins GM Andy MacPhail, and his roots in the broadcasting industry?

9.   How many saves did Jeff Reardon have in his first dozen games for the Twins in 1987?

10.   What was the team, inning and score when Joe Niekro was tossed out of the game for possessing sandpaper and an emery board?

11.   Who was the home plate umpire who ejected Niekro?

12.   When the Twins started Steve Carlton, Joe Niekro and Bert Blyleven against the Angels in a mid-August series, what was their combined major league experience?

13.   Who were the switch-hitters Twins manager Tom Kelly alternated as designated hitters late in the 1987 season?

14.   Whom did Bert Blyleven pass on the all-time strikeout list this season?

15. Who was the only Twins player to make the American League All-Star Game team in 1987?

16. How many first-round draft picks were on the Twins' 1987 roster?

17. How many of the 1987 Twins came to the team via trades?

18. How many of the Twins' 1987 pitchers were obtained via trades?

19. In how many consecutive games did Tim Laudner hit a home run when Joe Niekro was the Twins' starting pitcher?

20. What role did the Twins' pitching staff play in Don Mattingly's tie-making eight-consecutive-game home run record?

21. What did Kirby Puckett do in the 1987 All-Star Game?

22. In how many consecutive games did Bert Blyleven give up a home run before ending his streak June 15, 1987, against Milwaukee?

23. Can you name the principals in the trade that brought Dan Schatzeder to the Twins in 1987 from the Phillies?

24. When the Twins added Schatzeder and Joe Niekro during the 1987 season, what was the average age of their pitching staff?

25. Who are the Twins pitchers who are tied for second place in the all-time shutouts category behind Don Sutton?

26. What was the trade by which the Twins acquired Joe Niekro in 1987?

27. Who was the winning pitcher against the Kansas City Royals when the Twins jumped into first place in the AL-West for good?

28. How many switch-hitters did the Twins have on their 1987 roster?

29. Can you recall Tom Brunansky's torrid streak in May 1987 that raised his average some 41 points?

30. How many games has durable Gary Gaetti missed for the Twins over the past five seasons?

31. Can you name four of the nicknames commonly used in ESPN's reports of the Twins games by sportscaster Chris (Boomer) Berman?

32. Which Twins player was the first Columbia

University alumnus to appear in the major leagues since Lou Gehrig?

33. What former major league manager led three American League teams during his career and joined the Twins' front office in 1987?

34. What is the name of the fan who hangs the "Frankie Sweet Music Viola" sign in the dome, and what is his profession?

35. What was the name of the bride whose wedding Frank Viola had to miss because of his first-game World Series assignment?

36. Can you name the principals involved in the trade that brought Dan Gladden to the Twins?

37. What was the trade that brought relief pitcher Jeff Reardon from Montreal to the Twins?

38. What major league feat did Billy Beane commemorate in his first game after being called up from Portland during the last part of the 1987 season?

39. Within 15 wins and losses, what combined major league record did Steve Carlton and Joe Niekro bring to the Twins going into the 1987 season?

40. Which pitchers had the only shutouts on the Twins staff in 1987?

41. Which pitcher had the most complete games for the Twins in 1987?

42. Which pitcher worked the most innings for the Twins in 1987, and within 20 innings how many did he have?

43. How many saves did the Twins pitching staff produce in 1987?

44. How many wins did Frank Viola record in 1987, and what was his earned run average?

45. Who was the Twins' strikeout leader among its pitchers in 1987?

46. Which of the Twins was tied for the American League lead in base hits in 1987, and how many did he have?

47. Who was the Twins' stolen-base leader in 1987, and how many did he have?

48. Which Twins hitters drew the most walks in 1987, and within four, how many did he have?

49. How many Twins hit over .300 in 1987?

50.   Which Twins player had the most extra base hits in 1987, and how many did he have?

51.   Who was the only Twins player to drive in more than 100 runs in 1987, and how many did he have?

52.   Can you name the three Twins players who hit over 30 home runs in 1987?

53.   The Twins home field is artificial turf. What was their record on natural grass during the 1987 season?

54.   During the 1987 season, how many runs per game did the Twins average?

55.   Against what American League team did the Twins clinch their AL-West title, and who was the winning pitcher?

56.   What future Hall-of-Fame player did the Twins demote in order to make room for Don Baylor on the roster?

57.   What major league batting mark did Kirby Puckett tie in a two-game period, September 1-2?

58.   What was the fielding record that Gary Gaetti set for the Twins in 1987?

59. Which pitcher was the winner, and who got the save for the Twins in the final game of the AL playoffs?

60. How many combined years of major league experience do the two Niekro brothers enjoy, and how many World Series rosters was Joe Niekro on?

61. Who were the only Twins not to play against the Tigers in the AL playoffs?

62. Who led the Twins in hitting during the AL playoffs?

63. Twins shortstop Greg Gagne had as many extra base hits in the AL playoffs as Yankee shortstop Wayne Tolleson had for the entire 1987 season. How many?

64. Whose ninth-inning home run gave the Twins an edge in the final playoff game after they entered the inning with just a 6-4 lead?

65. Who made the final out in the fifth playoff game that gave the Twins the AL title?

66. Which Twins players drove in the four runs in the second inning of playoff game number 5?

67. Who drove in the eventual winning run in the Twins' third AL playoff victory over Detroit?

68. Who was at bat for the Tigers and who was pitching for the Twins when Tim Laudner picked off Darrell Evans at third base in the sixth inning of the fourth playoff game?

69. What Twins pitcher also pitched in the first game of the 1981 NL championship series?

70. How many times did Frank Viola pitch on three days rest in 1987, and what was his record?

71. Which Twins player drove in the winning run in the eighth inning of the first playoff game?

72. Who drove in, and who scored the tie-making run in the eighth inning of the first AL playoff game for the Twins?

73. Which Twins player became the first ever to hit homers in his first two league championship at-bats?

74. How many road games did the Twins win in 1987?

75. What was the Twins' number-one home record in the major leagues in 1987?

76. How many Twins players remained in 1987 from the 1982 team that won only 60 games?

77. Twins relief star Jeff Reardon once broke the strikeout record at the University of Massachusetts of what former Orioles ace?

78. Which major league team drafted Twins shortstop Greg Gagne?

79. Can you detail the trade that brought Greg Gagne to the Twins from the Yankees, and when the trade was made?

80. Who won the MVP award in the 1987 American League championship series?

81. When Bert Blyleven defeated the Tigers in the second game of the AL playoffs, he ended Jack Morris's winning streak at the Metrodome of how many games?

82. Where did Cards manager Whitey Herzog claim the Twins would finish if they played in the AL- or NL-East divisions?

83. When the Twins set a playoff record of 72 runs in 12 games, whose record did they beat and when was it established?

84. How many consecutive wins, regular and playoffs, did Frank Viola register in the Metrodome?

85. Who was the person wearing dark glasses shown in the picture taken with a group

of Twins and President Reagan following the World Series win?

86. What was the date of Frank Viola's last loss in the Metrodome in 1987?

87. What was Frank Viola's home record when his "Sweet Music" banner was unfurled?

88. What was the Twins' won-lost percentage during the 1987 season?

89. How did the Twins finish the last five games of the 1987 season?

90. How many games did the Twins win on the road after the All-Star break?

91. What was the Twins' record in the second half of the season (post All-Star Game break) and how many games in front of the AL-West did they finish?

92. What was the Twins' 1987 record at the All-Star break and how many games in first place were they in the AL-West?

Answers

1.   Viola finshed with a 2.90 ERA, second
     to Jimmy Key of Toronto among pitchers
     with 162 or more innings pitched.

2.   Pitchers George Frazier and Frank Viola,
     and infielder Roy Smalley all played in the
     College World Series.

3.   Relief pitcher Joe Klink and outfielder
     Mark Davidson

4.   Reardon mopped up for Frank Viola
     against the Oakland A's on April 8 and got
     credit for the save.

5.   Puckett homered in four straight games
     early in the 1987 season, one shy of Har-
     mon Killebrew's record.

6. Straker defeated Seattle, 6-1, with seven scoreless innings.

7. Puckett was leadoff hitter before Kelly placed him in the third spot.

8. MacPhail's dad, Lee, was president of the American League and a Yankees executive; his grandfather Larry owned the Yankees and Dodgers; and uncle Bill is VP of sports for Turner Broadcasting and was president of CBS Sports.

9. Reardon recorded 8 saves in his first 12 appearances.

10. Niekro was pitching against the Angels, with the score tied 2-2 in the fourth inning when he was ejected.

11. Tim Tschida

12. The three of them combined for 57 years of major league pitching experience.

13. Roy Smalley and Gene Larkin had the unusual role of being alternated as DH though each was a switch hitter. Smalley faced right-handers, Larkin lefties.

14. Blyleven moved past Ferguson Jenkins and into eighth place on the all time strikeout list.

15.   Kirby Puckett

16.   The Twins had only one first-round pick, Kirby Puckett.

17.   Thirteen

18.   The Twins had seven of their 10 hurlers via trade: Keith Atherton, Joe Niekro, Bert Blyleven, Jeff Reardon, Mike Smithson, George Frazier and Dan Schatzeder.

19.   In a most unusual streak, Laudner hit home runs in five consecutive games in 1987 in which Niekro was the starter.

20.   Mattingly started the streak with home runs off Twins pitchers Mike Smithson and Juan Berenguer on July 8, 1987.

21.   Puckett was 0-for-4 with one outfield putout after entering the game as a pinch-hitter for pitcher Jack Morris in the fifth inning.

22.   Blyleven had given up home runs in 20 consecutive games before blanking the Brewers, 5-0.

23.   The Twins got Schatzeder for minor league pitcher Danny Clay and third baseman Tom Schwarz.

24. The Twins pitching staff averaged almost 32 years of age.

25. Bert Blyleven and Steve Carlton each have 55 career shutouts, three behind Sutton.

26. The Twins traded catcher Mark Salas to the Yankees for Niekro on June 6, 1987.

27. Joe Niekro, just obtained from the Yankees, beat KC, 5-2, with 6⅔ innings pitched as part of a three-game sweep that put the Twins in first.

28. Three: Gene Larkin, Roy Smalley and Al Newman

29. Brunansky had 20 hits in 60 at-bats (.333), with five home runs and 17 RBIs, boosting his average at that time to .274.

30. Gaetti has missed just eight games.

31. Berman goes bonkers with Randy (Bird in the Hand) Bush; Dan (Man From) Gladden; Kirby (Union Gap) Puckett; and Frank (101 Strings) Viola.

32. Gene Larkin made his debut on May 21, 1987, ironically at first base. Gehrig's final game was in 1939.

33. Ralph Houk was a welcome addition to the Twins' front office in 1987.

34. Mark Dornfield, an assistant bowling alley manager in Bloomington, Minnesota, hangs Viola's favorite sign.

35. Donna Litt, who married Frank's brother John Viola

36. Gladden came from the Giants for Mickey Hatcher.

37. The Twins sent pitcher Neal Heaton and four other players for Reardon and catcher Tom Nieto.

38. Beane hit a single on the first pitch thrown to him for a game-winning RBI against Milwaukee.

39. Carlton was 323-229 and Niekro 213-190 for a combined mark of 536-419.

40. Frank Viola and Bert Blyleven had the only two shutouts by Twins pitchers in 1987.

41. Bert Blyleven had eight complete games for the Twins, and Frank Viola was second with seven.

42. Bert Blyleven led the Twins with 267 innings pitched.

43. Forty

44. Viola had 17 wins and a 2.90 ERA, both club highs.

45. Frank Viola led the club in strikeouts with 197, one more than Bert Blyleven.

46. Kirby Puckett tied Kevin Seitzer of the Royals with 207 hits.

47. Dan Gladden led the Twins base-stealers with 25.

48. Kent Hrbek led the Twins with 84 walks.

49. One—Kirby Puckett was the only Twins regular to bat over .300 with his .332 mark.

50. Gary Gaetti led the Twins with 69 extra base hits, including 36 doubles, two triples and 31 homers.

51. Tom Brunansky drove in 104.

52. Kent Hrbek (34), Tom Brunansky (32) and Gary Gaetti (31)

53. The Twins won 24 and lost 38 games on natural grass.

54. Five

55. The Twins defeated the Texas Rangers, 5-3, on September 28, 1987, and reliever Juan Berenguer was the winner in relief of Joe Niekro.

56. The Twins sent pitcher Steve Carlton to Portland (PCL) for 24 hours and made Baylor eligible for the playoffs.

57. Puckett got 10 hits in consecutive nine-inning games to tie Reggie Stennett's major league record and set an AL mark.

58. Gaetti went 47 games without committing an error at third base, a club record.

59. Bert Blyleven was the winning pitcher and Jeff Reardon got the save.

60. The Niekros, Phil and Joe, have a combined 45 years major league experience. Joe was on his third Series roster in 1987.

61. Joe Niekro, Roy Smalley and George Frazier

62. Tom Brunansky led the Twins in the playoffs with a .412 average.

63. Gagne had five extra base hits.

64. Tom Brunansky hit a one-out home run for a 7-4 lead.

65. Twins reliever Jeff Reardon threw out Detroit catcher Matt Nokes on a weak grounder.

66. Tom Brunansky's double scored Gary Gaetti and Randy Bush; Dan Gladden singled home Steve Lombardozzi; and Kirby Puckett singled home Gladden.

67. Greg Gagne broke a 1-1 tie in the fourth inning with a home run, giving the Twins a lead they never lost.

68. Juan Berneguer was pitching to Lou Whitaker and Laudner picked off Evans on the first pitch.

69. Jeff Reardon pitched for Montreal against the Dodgers in 1981.

70. Viola pitched three times on three days rest during the 1987 season, with a 1-1 mark.

71. Don Baylor hit a bases-loaded single off Willie Hernandez and drove in Kirby Puckett from third base.

72. Kirby Puckett doubled home Dan Gladden to tie the score 5-5 in the eighth inning.

73. Gary Gaetti

74. The Twins had a major league low of 29 road wins.

75. The Twins had a 56-25 home record.

76. Six players: Frank Viola, Kent Hrbek, Randy Bush, Tim Laudner, Tom Brunansky, and Gary Gaetti

77. Mike Flanagan

78. The Yankees drafted Gagne and later traded him to the Twins.

79. In 1982 Gagne came to the Twins with Ron Davis and Paul Boris for Gary Serum and Roy Smalley.

80. Gary Gaetti

81. Morris was 11-0 at the Dome before that game.

82. Fourth

83. The Twins broke the Red Sox' 1986 record of 68 runs in 14 games.

84. Eleven

85. Former Twins pitcher Steve Carlton

86. May 22

87.   17-0

88.   .525, lowest ever for a World Series champion

89.   They lost all five.

90.   Nine

91.   36-36, and two games ahead

92.   85-77, and one game up

World Series

1. How many home runs did the Twins hit in the 1987 World Series?

2. Who hit grand slam homers for the Twins in the World Series?

3. When the Twins hit two grand slam homers in the World Series, whose record did they tie?

4. Who were the switch-hitters in the regular St. Louis Cardinals lineup?

5. What was the right-handed average of the Cards' switch-hitters against Twins lefties in the World Series?

6. What was the score in the sixth game of the World Series when Don Baylor cracked his two-run homer?

7. What was the combined score of the Twins' three losses in St. Louis?

8. Which seven-game starting player for the Twins had the highest batting average, and what was it?

9. Which Twins players led the team in extra-base hits during the World Series?

10. Which Twins player had the most hits for the World Series, and how many did he have?

11. Which Twins player drove in the most runs, and how many RBIs did he have?

12. Three Twins players tied for the most runs with five. Who were they?

13. How many triples did the Cardinals, known for their great base-running speed, accumulate during the World Series against the Twins?

14. Who were the only Cardinals to hit home runs off the Twins' pitchers?

15. How did the Twins and Cardinals compare in team batting averages for the seven World Series games?

16. Who were the four Twins starters who batted over .300 during the World Series?

17. What Cardinal pitchers defeated the Twins in the World Series?

18. Which pitcher accumulated the most strikeouts during the World Series?

19. What Twins pitchers were forced to hit during the three games at St. Louis, and how did they do?

20. Who were the two Cardinals used as designated hitters during the World Series?

21. Which Cards hitter led his team in batting during the World Series?

22. Which Cardinal player had the most hits during the World Series?

23. What was the count on Don Baylor when he hit the two-run homer that tied the sixth game, 5-5?

24. Who singled home the tie-breaking and eventual winning run in the fifth inning of Game 6?

25. How did Tom Brunansky advance to second base just before he was driven home for the game-tying run in the fifth inning of Game 6?

26. What was Kent Hrbek's record against left-handed pitchers in the Series prior to his grand slam home run in the sixth game against Ken Dayley?

27. What was the count when Kent Hrbek hit his grand slam homer in the sixth game?

28. How many Twins hit balls out of the in-field in the sixth inning of Game 6 prior to Kent Hrbek's grand slam homer?

29. Who drove in the Twins' only run in their 3-1 loss to the Cards in Game 3?

30. What was the count on Greg Gagne when he hit his home run for a 1-0 Twins lead in Game 4?

31. How did the Twins score their two runs in Game 5?

32. How many World Series games had Tom Kelly, Twins manager, attended before leading his team in the 1987 Series?

33. Why was the number 4 especially significant for Kirby Puckett in the Twins' sixth-game victory?

34. What were the fewest runs the Twins scored at the Metrodome during the AL Playoffs and World Series?

35.   What was the Twins' batting mark, home run numbers and how many runs and hits did they accumulate in their three World Series games in St. Louis?

36.   How many home runs did the Twins hit in the Metrodome during the World Series?

37.   Situation in Game 7: Greg Gagne hit a grounder to Cards first baseman, who tossed to pitcher Joe Magrane covering the bag. What happened on the play?

38.   Which Twins were credited with game-winning RBIs during the World Series?

39.   What was the full-share payoff to each of the Twins players for their World Series victory?

40.   Who was the World Series Most Valuable Player?

41.   Name the home plate umpire in Game 7 of the World Series who was involved in a pair of controversial decisions.

42.   What was the final out in Game 7 of the World Series?

43.   Who accounted for the winning run in the Twins' seventh-game victory over St. Louis?

44. Who scored the tie-breaking run for the Twins in the sixth inning of Game 7?

45. Name the Cardinals runner who was picked off first base by Twins pitcher Frank Viola, snuffing out St. Louis's final rally.

46. Name the National League umpire who ruled Tommy Herr out at first base when Frank Viola picked him off on a controversial play.

47. What was the Twins' record-setting worst earned run average for a World Series winner?

48. Who was the losing Cardinals pitcher in the seventh game?

49. What Cardinals pitcher gave up the winning hit in the sixth inning of Game 7?

50. Who were the Twins' baserunners in the sixth inning of Game 7 when the winning run scored?

51. How did the three Twins baserunners get on in the sixth inning of the seventh game prior to the game-winning hit?

52. Who made the two outs in the sixth inning for the Twins prior to the winning run scoring in Game 7?

53. What was the count when Greg Gagne hit his game-winning single in the sixth inning of Game 7?

54. Who was the Cardinals' third baseman who fielded Greg Gagne's game-winning hit in the sixth inning of Game 7?

55. Who scored the final Twins run in the eighth inning of Game 7?

56. Who drove in the final run in the Twins 4-2 seventh game victory?

57. What Twins pitcher was the first to warm up when the Cardinals got their two runs in the second inning of Game 7?

58. Which Twins hitter drove in the first run in Game 7?

59. Who scored the Twins' first run in Game 7?

60. Which Twins player scored the tie-making run in the fifth inning of Game 7?

61. Who drove in the tie-making run in the fifth inning of Game 7 for the Twins, and how did he do it?

62. Which Twins player was thrown out at home plate in the fifth inning of Game 7?

63. How many saves did Jeff Reardon accumulate in the World Series?

64. What was the margin by which the Twins outscored the Cardinals in the World Series?

65. How many hits did Frank Viola allow in winning Game 1?

66. How many days rest did Viola have when he won Game 7?

67. How many hits, runs and innings pitched did Frank Viola record when he lost Game 4 to the Cardinals?

68. What was Frank Viola's won-lost record during the regular season when he pitched on three days rest?

69. How many hits did Frank Viola allow in winning the seventh game of the World Series?

70. This Cardinals player was the first to be ejected from a World Series game since Joaquin Andujar of the Cardinals in 1985. Who was he?

71. Which pitcher became the first rookie ever to start the first and last games of a World Series without a start in any of the other five games?

72. Which Twins hitter had reached base six consecutive times before lining out to Willie McGee in the third inning of Game 7?

73. Who threw out the first ball prior to Game 7 of the World Series?

74. Who were the other Twins pitchers besides Frank Viola to win games during the World Series?

75. Which Twins starter had the lowest earned run mark during the World Series?

76. What home run record in the World Series did Dan Gladden and Ken Hrbek tie?

77. Which Twins players had World Series experience before 1987, and for whom did they play?

78. How many hits by the Cardinals produced their two runs in the second inning of Game No. 7?

Answers

1. Six

2. Dan Gladden and Kent Hrbek

3. The 1956 New York Yankees (against Brooklyn)

4. Willie McGee, Vince Coleman, Ozzie Smith, Tom Herr and Jose Oquendo

5. A paltry 9-for-50, or .180

6. The Cardinals led, 5-3.

7. 14-5 in favor of St. Louis

8. Kirby Puckett, .357

9.   Dan Gladden and Gary Gaetti, four each

10. Kirby Puckett, 10

11. Dan Gladden, seven

12. Kirby Puckett, Tom Brunansky and Greg Gagne

13. None

14. Tom Lawless and Tommy Herr

15. The Twins outhit the Cards, .269 to .259.

16. Steve Lombardozzi (.412), Don Baylor (.385), Kirby Puckett (.357) and Tim Laudner (.318)

17. John Tudor (Game 3), Bob Forsch (Game 4) and Danny Cox (Game 5)

18. Twins lefty Frank Viola, 16

19. Les Straker (0-for-2), Bert Blyleven (0-for-1) and Frank Viola (0-for-1)

20. Terry Pendleton and Tom Pagnozzi

21. Catcher Tony Pena, .409

22. Willie McGee, 10

23. He hit the first pitch from John Tudor.

24. Tom Lombardozzi's single scored Tom Brunansky for a 6-5 Twins lead.

25. On a fielder's choice as Tim Laudner bounced to pitcher Rich Horton, who elected to make the play at first base

26. 0-for-16

27. He hit Dayley's first pitch.

28. None: Gagne got an infield hit; Kirby Puckett walked on four pitches; and Don Baylor was intentially passed.

29. Tom Brunansky's 2-2, broken bat single scored Greg Gagne in the sixth inning.

30. 2-0 with Bob Forsch pitching

31. Gary Gaetti tripled on a 2-2 pitch with Dan Gladden and Greg Gagne on base.

32. None. The first one he ever saw was the opening game of the 1987 Series.

33. He had four hits in four at-bats and scored four runs.

34. Four, in the seventh game of the World Series

35. They batted .184, with one HR, five runs and 18 hits.

36. Six

37. Magrane missed the bag with his right foot but caught it with a sweeping reverse pivot with his left before Gagne arrived. Umpire Lee Weyer called Gagne safe.

38. Kent Hrbek (Game 1), Gary Gaetti (Game 2), Tom Lombardozzi (Game 6) and Greg Gagne (Game 7)

39. $85,580.97 per full share

40. Twins pitcher Frank Viola

41. Dave Phillips

42. Gary Gaetti threw out Willie McGee at first base.

43. Greg Gagne hit a bases-loaded single in the sixth inning, driving in a run that broke a 2-2 tie.

44. Tom Brunansky

45. Tommy Herr

46. Lee Weyer

47. 4.63

48. Danny Cox

49. Todd Worrell

50. Tom Brunansky was on third, Kent Hrbek was on second, and Roy Smalley on first.

51. All three walked.

52. Tim Laudner popped up and Dan Gladden struck out.

53. 3 and 2

54. Tom Lawless

55. Tim Laudner

56. Dan Gladden, on a double

57. Bert Blyleven

58. Steve Lombardozzi, with a single

59. Tom Brunansky

60. Greg Gagne

61. Kirby Puckett doubled to right-center.

62. Gary Gaetti was thrown out by Greg Coleman as he tried to score from second base.

63.   One, in Game 7

64.   38-26

65.   Five

66.   Three

67.   Five runs and six hits in 3⅓ innings

68.   2-2

69.   Six hits in eight innings

70.   St. Louis pitcher Danny Cox in the sixth inning of Game 7

71.   Joe Magrane of the Cardinals

72.   Kirby Puckett, on five singles and a walk

73.   Former Twins owner Calvin Griffith, former president Howard Fox and current owner Carl Pohlad

74.   Bert Blyleven and Dan Schatzeder

75.   Bert Blyleven (2.77)

76.   Gladden and Hrbek became the first pair of teammates since Yogi Berra and Moose Skowron of the Yankees to hit grand slam home runs.

77.   George Frazier, Dodgers, 1981; Bert Blyleven, Pirates, 1979; and Juan Berenguer, Padres, 1984, though he did not get into a game.

78.   Four singles, by Jim Lindemann, Tim McGee, Tony Pena and Steve Lake

Miscellaneous

1. What was the lowest batting average ever to lead the Twins in a single season, and who was the player?

2. Who hit the fewest home runs to lead the team in a single season, and what was that number?

3. Which player led the Twins with the fewest number of RBIs for a single season and what was that number?

4. During the Twins' existence, how many native Minnesotans have played for the team?

5. Which Twins minor league team has been a part of its developmental organization

for the most consecutive seasons?

6. Who is the only Twins player ever to lead the team in batting, homers and RBIs in a single season?

7. In 1986, when Al Woods was used as a pinch-hitter only in games against the Brewers, Yankees and Rangers, what record did he set?

8. Who is the only Twins hitter ever to have a perfect season against one opponent in more than two at-bats?

9. Can you name the most successful calendar date for the Twins? What happened to them on that date in 1987?

10. What is the Twins' record for most consecutive pinch-hitters in one game? Who was the manager at the time?

11. Which state has produced the most players for the Twins?

12. Though he lives in New Jersey in the off-season, Twins manager Tom Kelly is a native of which Minnesota town?

13. Who was the first native Minnesotan ever to become a member of the team's managerial staff?

14. During seven seasons as a manager in both the major and minor leagues, how many losing seasons has Tom Kelly endured?

15. Tom Kelly is the second native Minnesotan ever to manager a major league team, but who was the first?

16. Who are the only managers ever to take the Twins to a first-place finish, in either the former league champion format or the divisional format?

17. How many former Twins players have also managed the team?

18. In what year was Tony Oliva selected as the Rookie of the Year in the American League?

19. Which player has appeared in the most regular-season games in one season in Twins history?

20. Now that Don Baylor, the majors' all-time leader in being hit by a pitch, is on the team, what record by Cesar Tovar is in jeopardy?

21. Who holds the Twins' record for fewest strikeouts in a single season, based on 500 or more at-bats?

22. Which Twins player was the least likely to hit into double plays during a single season?

23. Who is the Twins' single-season stolen bases leader?

24. In his rookie 1984 season, Kirby Puckett had 24 bunt hits. How many homers did he hit?

25. Which Twins player has the club record for most seasons with the team?

26. Which player spent the most *full* seasons with the Twins?

27. Who has played the most games in Twins history?

28. Which Twins player holds the team record for being hit by pitches *while with the team*?

29. Which Twins player struck out the most during his career?

30. Which Twins player holds the club record for drawing the most walks?

31. Which Twins player grounded into the most double plays?

32. Which Twins player had the most career sacrifice flies?

33. Who is the Twins' all-time stolen bases leader?

34. Counting the Twins' World Series win, how many different teams have now been crowned world champion over the past ten Series?

35. In 1956 and 1957, current Cardinals manager Whitey Herzog played centerfield for the Senators between which left- and right-fielder?

36. The Twins hope to become the first team to repeat as World Champions in 1988 since which team turned the feat, and when?

37. Who is older, Twins DH Don Baylor or Twins GM Andy McPhail?

38. Who were the first Twins players ever involved in a trade?

39. Billy Martin came to the Twins in a 1961 trade for what player?

40. Who were the two future Twins managers once involved in deals within 14 days of each other?

41. What Twins player holds the distinction of being traded for the most people?

42. Who were the players involved when Rod Carew was traded to the California Angels in 1979?

43. Whom did the Twins give up to get Jim Perry from the Cleveland Indians in 1963?

44. Can you name the deal that brought pitcher Jim "Mudcat" Grant to the Twins in 1964?

45. Who were the only two native Minnesotans on the Twins' first 1961 team?

46. Which two Twins players came to the team in 1987 for a price tag of ten dollars each?

47. In what season did the Twins become only one of three teams in major league history to have six 20-homer producers?

48. Who was the first winner of the Calvin R. Griffith award given annually to the Twins' MVP?

49. Who is the only Twins player to win the Calvin R. Griffith award as the team's MVP six straight years, and what were the years?

50. Who was the first winner of the Bill Boni award, given to the Twins' outstanding rookie player?

51. Who were the three Twins players elected as Rookie of the Year in the American League and what were the years?

52. Strange as it may seem, this player twice won the Charles O. Johnson award given to the "most improved Twin."

53. Who is the only player to be chosen as the Twins' most improved player for two consecutive seasons?

54. Harmon Killebrew certainly was best known as a power hitter; in how many seasons did he fail to steal a base?

55. Which Twins catcher has the best single-season fielding mark?

56. Which Twins player had the highest percentage of successful stolen bases in one season?

57. Who was the former Minnesota All-America football star, and later athletic director at the university, who was a pitcher on the first Twins team?

58. Which opposing pitcher had the most one-hitters against the Twins?

59.   Which three pitchers hurled no-hitters against the Twins?

60.   Who is the only pitcher ever to hurl a perfect game against the Twins?

61.   Which Twins hitter was the biggest spoiler of no-hitters?

Answers

1. John Castino's .268 mark was the best on the Twins in 1981.

2. Roy Smalley's seven home runs in the strike-shortened season of 1981 topped the Twins.

3. Mickey Hatcher had 37 RBIs in 1981, the strike season, to lead the Twins.

4. Sixteen Twins players have been Minnesota natives.

5. Orlando begins its 26th straight year as a Twins farm club in 1988.

6. John Castino was the team's only triple crown winner in 1980 with a .302 average, 13 homers and 64 RBIs.

7. Woods is the only Twins player ever to go 5-for-5 as a pinch hitter against three teams.

8. In 1972, Jim Holt went three-for-three in his only game that year against the Angels.

9. July 13 has been best for the Twins with a 15-3 record (.833), but it didn't matter in 1987 since it was part of the All-Star break.

10. The Twins sent seven consecutive PHs to the plate against Seattle on August 6, 1979, when Gene Mauch was manager.

11. Fifty-eight Twins players were born in California, tops among all 50 states.

12. He was born in Graceville, Minnesota, on August 15, 1950.

13. Current manager Tom Kelly, when appointed as a coach in 1983

14. None, including his 12-11 record in finishing the 1986 season as Twins skipper

15. A. M. Thompson, a St. Paul native, managed his city's team in the 1884 Union Association, then a recognized "major" league.

16. Sam Mele (1965), Billy Martin (1969), Bill Rigney (1970) and Tom Kelly (1987)

17. Four: Billy Martin (played in 1961), Frank Quilici (played in 1965, 1967-1970), Johnny Goryl (played in 1962-1964) and Tom Kelly (played in 1975)

18. 1964

19. Cesar Tovar, 164 games in 1967, a league-leading figure that year

20. Tovar holds the single-season Twins record of being hit—17 times in 1968.

21. Vic Power struck out just 24 times during 541 at-bats in 1963.

22. Cesar Tovar hit into only two in 1968.

23. Rod Carew had 49 in 1976.

24. None

25. Tony Oliva, 15

26. Harmon Killebrew, 14

27.   Harmon Killebrew, 1,939

28.   Cesar Tovar, 68

29.   Harmon Killebrew, 1,314

30.   Harmon Killebrew, 1,321

31.   Harmon Killebrew, 210

32.   Harmon Killebrew, 66

33.   Rod Carew, 271

34.   Ten, from 1978 to 1987

35.   Jim Lemon and Roy Sievers

36.   The Yankees were the last team to win back-to-back championships—in 1977-1978.

37.   Baylor was 38 at the end of the 1987 season; McPhail was 34.

38.   Third baseman Reno Bertoia and pitcher Paul Giel were traded to Kansas City for outfielder Bill Tuttle on June 1, 1961.

39.   Shortstop Billy Consolo

40.   Billy Martin for Billy Consolo of the Milwaukee Braves on June 1, 1961, and

Billy Gardner for pitcher Danny McDevitt of the Yankees on June 14, 1961

41. Pitcher Bert Blyleven was involved in two deals that involved nine other players.

42. The Twins received pitchers Paul Hartzell and Brad Havens, catcher Dave Engle and outfielder Ken Landreaux.

43. Pitcher Jack Kralick

44. Third baseman George Banks and pitcher Lee Stange were sent to Cleveland for Grant on June 15, 1964.

45. Pitchers Frank Bruchbauer and Paul Giel

46. Roy Smalley and Joe Niekro

47. 1964

48. Harmon Killebrew, 1961

49. Rod Carew, 1972-1977

50. Bernie Albers, 1962

51. Tony Oliva, 1964; Rod Carew, 1967; John Castino, 1979

52. Rod Carew (1969 and 1977)

53.   Ted Uhlaender (1967 and 1968)

54.   Killebrew holds the AL record for not stealing a base in three seasons in which he appeared in 150 or more games.

55.   Glenn Borgmann made only two errors in 704 total chances in 1974 for a .997 mark to lead all Twins catchers.

56.   Gary Ward stole 13 bases in 14 tries in 1982 for a .929 success rate.

57.   Paul Giel was a former All-America football star, and later AD for the Gophers who pitched for the Twins in 1961.

58.   Jim Palmer of the Orioles pitched two one-hitters against the Twins, in 1976 and 1982.

59.   Jim Hunter and Vida Blue of the A's, and Nolan Ryan of the Angels pitched no-hitters against the Twins.

60.   Jim (Catfish) Hunter had a perfect game for the A's against the Twins on May 8, 1968, and beat them, 4-0.

61.   Cesar Tovar had the only hit in four games for the Twins, spoiling a pair of no-hitters for both the Orioles and Senators.

Photographs

1. This man, now a Twins broadcaster, played left field, third base and first base during his career. Who is he?

National Baseball Library, Cooperstown, NY

2. This infielder was the only Twins regular to hit a grand slam home run during the pennant-winning 1965 season. Identify him.

National Baseball Library, Cooperstown, NY

3.   What is Tony Oliva's real first name?

National Baseball Library, Cooperstown, NY

4. This Twins infielder played for 10 seasons and finished his career with a .260 lifetime batting average. Who is he?

National Baseball Library, Cooperstown, NY

5.   What was Jim Kaat's career ERA, com-
     piled over 13 seasons?

National Baseball Library, Cooperstown, NY

6.   Name this Twins left-hander, who had a
        better than two-to-one ratio of strikeouts
        to walks in his Twins career.

National Baseball Library, Cooperstown, NY

7.   Where does Jim Perry rank in innings
     pitched among all Twins pitchers?

National Baseball Library, Cooperstown, NY

8. This great Twins contract hitter smacked how many home runs during his Twins career?

St. Paul Pioneer Press Dispatch

9.   This player reached first base on a catch-
     er's interference 11 times in 1984 while
     playing with Toledo of the International
     League. Who is he?

145

St. Paul Pioneer Press Dispatch

10. How many home runs did this Twins catcher have in spite of hitting only .191 during the 1987 season?

St. Paul Pioneer Press Dispatch

11.   Who is this player, who won the J. Roy
        Stockton award for Outstanding Achieve-
        ment in Baseball from the St. Louis
        Baseball Writers Association in 1986?

St. Paul Pioneer Press Dispatch

12.   Can you spell Bert Blyleven's given name?

St. Paul Pioneer Press Dispatch

13.   In 1986 this player led the Twins with six
      bunt hits and 13 sacrifice bunts. Who is he?

St. Paul Pioneer Press Dispatch

14. Name this pitcher, who played for nine minor league teams in ten seasons before making the Twins' varsity in 1987.

St. Paul Pioneer Press Dispatch

15.   This DH helped the Boston Red Sox win
       the 1986 American League pennant.
       Who is he?

St. Paul Pioneer Press Dispatch

16.   With what team did Jeff Reardon begin
       his major league career?

St. Paul Pioneer Press Dispatch

17. In 1987 Tom Brunansky had exactly the same numbers for home runs and RBIs as he had in 1984. What were they?

18.   Kent Hrbek had his highest home run
       figures in 1987 since turning professional.
       How many did he hit?

St. Paul Pioneer Press Dispatch

19. What college did Kirby Puckett attend before signing with the Twins?

Answers

1.   Harmon Killebrew

2.   Zoilo Versalles

3.   Pedro

4.   Rich Reese

5.   3.28

6.   Mudcat Grant

7.   Third

8.   Seventy-four

9.   Steve Lombardozzi

Photographs—Answers

10. Sixteen

11. Gary Gaetti

12. Rik Aalbert

13. Greg Gagne

14. Les Straker

15. Don Baylor

16. The New York Mets

17. 32 homers and 85 RBIs

18. Thirty-four

19. Bradley University